Es_____ __ ____

From:

Date:

My Prayer JOURNAL

c~s~c

Serenity for a Woman's Soul

BARBOUR BOOKS

An Imprint of Barbour Publishing, Inc.

© 2019 by Barbour Publishing, Inc.

Compiled by Kathy Shutt.

Prayers by Emily Biggers and Valorie Quesenberry.

ISBN 978-1-68322-943-8

Published by Barbour Books, an imprint of Barbour Publishing, Inc., 1810 Barbour Drive, Uhrichsville, Ohio 44683, www.barbourbooks.com

Our mission is to inspire the world with the life-changing message of the Bible.

Member of the
Evangelical Christian
Publishers Association

Printed in China.

Introduction

Draw nigh to God, and he will draw nigh to you.
JAMES 4:8 KJV

As women living out our faith in an increasingly busy world, it's so important to spend time each day in the presence of our loving Creator. *My Prayer Journal: Serenity for a Woman's Soul* is a collection of prayer starters and scripture selections designed to help you set aside daily quiet time and soak in the heavenly Father's loving presence as you begin a purposeful conversation with Him. As you read through the prayers and meditate on the scripture selections, journal your own prayers and praises in the generous space provided. Be blessed!

Content with My Appearance

God, there is such order, yet such creativity in all You have made. Such beauty. Such precision. Such forethought. There is no way that this world just appeared. It was designed by You, sovereign God. You are good. You created the trees in all their splendor, the mighty oceans white with foam, and the vast array of animal life. How could I ignore the fact that You also created me so beautifully?

"Has anyone by fussing in front of the mirror ever gotten taller by so much as an inch? All this time and money wasted on fashion—do you think it makes that much difference? Instead of looking at the fashions, walk out into the fields and look at the wildflowers. They never primp or shop, but have you ever seen color and design quite like it?"
MATTHEW 6:27–29 MSG

_____

_____

_____

_____

_____

_____

_____

_____

_____

_____

A Masterpiece Created by God

Heavenly Father, thank You for making me exactly who I am. You created me and knit me together in my mother's womb. You know me inside and out. I often wish I weren't so complicated. Sometimes my feelings get hurt too easily. . .and I feel like I'm not talented enough at many things. But then I remember that to criticize myself is really an insult to You. You made me, and You created a masterpiece when You did.

Thank you for making me so wonderfully complex!
Your workmanship is marvelous—how well I know it.
PSALM 139:14 NLT

_____

_____

_____

_____

_____

_____

_____

_____

_____

_____

_____

_____

Set Free

Dear Father God, I imagine the slaves who were set free after the Civil War. How strange it must have felt to be imprisoned by a master one minute and set free as an independent human being the next! I have experienced a similar freeing through Christ. I once was bound by sin and darkness. My soul was bound for hell. There was no way I could come before You in all of Your holiness. I was stained with sin so deep and dark that there was no chance for me. But when I invited Jesus into my heart, I was set free.

Therefore, there is now no condemnation for those who are in Christ Jesus, because through Christ Jesus the law of the Spirit who gives life has set you free from the law of sin and death.
Romans 8:1–2 niv

_____

_____

_____

_____

_____

_____

_____

_____

_____

_____

Live at Peace

Heavenly Father, I think the inability to live at peace with others comes down to selfishness. I get so caught up in myself sometimes that I am unable to see the bigger picture. Just because someone hurts me, I don't have to react in anger or retaliation. Just because I disagree, I don't have to argue or tear someone else down in order to promote my opinion. Just because I may be right, I don't have to push my agenda on others. There is a better way. It is the way Jesus showed us when He walked on earth.

If it is possible, as far as it depends on you, live at peace with everyone.
ROMANS 12:18 NIV

Love One Another

God of Love, I come before You now, and I feel ashamed. I am sorry that so many times my words are not spoken in love. My actions are not always a reflection of love either. My heart, at times, is filled with anger or disgust and packed so tightly with these emotions that there is no room left for love. Help me to see my family through Your eyes, Father. Help me to see my coworkers and friends through Your lens of love.

"A new command I give you: Love one another. As I have loved you, so you must love one another. By this everyone will know that you are my disciples, if you love one another."
JOHN 13:34–35 NIV

_____

_____

_____

_____

_____

_____

_____

_____

_____

_____

_____

Relating to My Parents

God, please help me to honor my parents. Show me what honoring them means, now that I am a grown woman and they are growing older. Show me how to treat my parents with respect, no matter what. They are a blessing to me, chosen by You to be some of the closest people in my life. I love them, Father, and I want to honor You in how I relate to them.

"Honor your father and your mother, so that you may live long in the land the LORD your God is giving you."
EXODUS 20:12 NIV

Be Found Trustworthy

God, I know that being found trustworthy is of extreme importance. I think of the great men and women of the Bible who were upright and of good character. Lord, teach me to concentrate fully on doing Your will. Help me to be found trustworthy, not only by others, but by You, my God. I want to be someone whom others can trust. Help me to avoid idleness and gossip. Neither brings blessing or serenity to my relationships.

A gossip betrays a confidence, but a trustworthy person keeps a secret.
PROVERBS 11:13 NIV

Be Still and Know

Heavenly Father, as I enter into this quiet time with You, I ask that You help me to remember You are still God and You are still in control. As I still my heart before You and open Your Word, lead me to the right scriptures and the right messages from You. Clear my mind of all the distractions that fight for my attention. Help me to find peaceful moments alone with You, in which You can encourage and strengthen me. I need You so.

He says, "Be still, and know that I am God; I will be exalted among the nations, I will be exalted in the earth."
PSALM 46:10 NIV

_____

_____

_____

_____

_____

_____

_____

_____

_____

_____

_____

_____

Early in the Morning

Jesus, You set an example for me. I read in the book of Mark that You went off alone to pray in a solitary place. You went early in the morning. You didn't wait until you fell into bed, exhausted, at the end of a long day. You sought Your heavenly Father in prayer first thing. Before the cock crowed. Before the world woke up. Before the busyness of day-to-day life began. This is the example You set for me, and this is the example I will follow. I want to honor You in all I do, including how I begin my day.

Very early in the morning, while it was still dark, Jesus got up, left the house and went off to a solitary place, where he prayed.
MARK 1:35 NIV

_____

_____

_____

_____

_____

_____

_____

_____

_____

_____

_____

Fellowship with God

I am so blessed, Lord, that You have come into my life. You knocked at the door of my heart. I remember the day. I remember life on my own, before I knew You—before You came into my heart and began to walk with me, doing life with me, guiding me in Your ways. Those were not my best days, God. These—with You—are. I have the privilege of fellowshipping with the Creator of the universe. I get to visit with the Great I Am. May I never take this privilege for granted or forget with whom I speak.

Here I am! I stand at the door and knock. If anyone hears my voice and opens the door, I will come in and eat with that person, and they with me.
REVELATION 3:20 NIV

Rest in the Lord

God, this world is busy. We find ways to occupy our every waking minute. Work dominates our days and nights. We busy ourselves with hobbies and meetings and even entertainment. Father, You are my only source of true rest. When my head hits the pillow tonight, may I be found faithful. May I seek You even in my rest. May I commit my soul to You even as I sleep. You are my salvation and my joy. You are my strength and my serenity.

Truly my soul finds rest in God; my salvation comes from him.
PSALM 62:1 NIV

Peace in My Prayers

God, I come to You in this secret place. I have withdrawn from the world and all its busyness in order to hear You speak. I seek You here in private. Just the two of us. I speak words of praise and thanksgiving. I present requests to You for my own needs and the needs of others. I ask Your forgiveness for my sins—not just in general, but for specific sins that come to mind as I pray. Help me to always find such peaceful, quiet times to withdraw from all the responsibilities of the day and simply meet with my Father.

But when you pray, go into your room, close the door
and pray to your Father, who is unseen. Then your Father,
who sees what is done in secret, will reward you.
MATTHEW 6:6 NIV

Housework

Father God, I just can't imagine that washing dishes and doing laundry can bring You glory! Does driving the carpool and making spaghetti for dinner mean anything to You? Surely not, I would think! But then I read about the Proverbs 31 woman, and I find her busy about household chores. I want to be such a woman, Lord. Show me how to make the most of my time and to be organized in my approach to household tasks.

She carefully watches everything in her household
and suffers nothing from laziness.
PROVERBS 31:27 NLT

Avoiding Shortcuts

God, I've learned the hard way that shortcuts are not all they're cracked up to be! Often, when I try to take the easy way out or the easiest path, things don't turn out so great. I ask that You would help me to be a good planner and a hard worker. Show me the work cut out for me, and help me to accomplish those tasks in a way that pleases You.

Good planning and hard work lead to prosperity,
but hasty shortcuts lead to poverty.
PROVERBS 21:5 NLT

Peace in My Church

God, Your Church has always been important to You, from the very start. You are our Great Shepherd; and when we gather together to worship You, You find it pleasing. I ask You, Father, to grant me serenity in my church. The members of this wonderful community bless me in so many ways. There are times, though, when I grow frustrated. Each member is a blessing and is so special to You. Help us to see one another as You see us, Lord. Help us to value each other's opinions and ways.

"Now I say to you that you are Peter (which means 'rock'), and upon this rock I will build my church, and all the powers of hell will not conquer it."
MATTHEW 16:18 NLT

Your Will for My Life

God, fill my thoughts with understanding. I know that when I am able to comprehend Your will for my life, I will follow gladly in Your ways. I want to please You with all of my thoughts. I make a lot of plans for my own life, but I pray that I will always be attentive to the signs and factors that You use to direct me. Help me to put Your ways into practice with all of my heart.

Give me understanding and I will obey your instructions;
I will put them into practice with all my heart.
PSALM 119:34 NLT

Precious Promises

The Bible is full of Your promises, Lord. There is one for every event, emotion, and season of my life. Believers of every age have stood firm on these promises and had the strength to weather temptation, face persecution, endure grief, and triumph over every obstacle they encountered. Thank You for filling the pages of scripture with such beautiful assurances of Your presence and power. It blesses me to know I can turn to them in times of need.

He has given us his very great and precious promises.
2 PETER 1:4 NIV

_____

_____

_____

_____

_____

_____

_____

_____

_____

_____

_____

_____

Think on Noble Things

Heavenly Father, may my thought life be pure, and may it honor You, my God. So many times my thoughts drift to selfish pursuits. Help me to focus on praising You. You are great and greatly to be praised. Bring to mind all that I have been blessed with so that I will be filled with a grateful heart.

Finally, brothers and sisters, whatever is true, whatever is noble, whatever is right, whatever is pure, whatever is lovely, whatever is admirable— if anything is excellent or praiseworthy—think about such things.
PHILIPPIANS 4:8 NIV

_____

_____

_____

_____

_____

_____

_____

_____

_____

_____

_____

_____

_____

_____

Renew My Mind

Renew my mind, heavenly Father, so that my thoughts might please You and my actions reflect Your great love. As a believer in Christ Jesus, just as believers who have gone before me, I must not conform to the ways of this world. Show me a different way, Lord. Illuminate the path before me and shine Your light into the recesses of my mind. In those times when I am tempted to go the way of the world, draw me back, I pray.

Do not conform to the pattern of this world, but be transformed by the renewing of your mind. Then you will be able to test and approve what God's will is—his good, pleasing and perfect will.
ROMANS 12:2 NIV

_____

_____

_____

_____

_____

_____

_____

_____

_____

_____

Jesus Wept

Jesus, You wept. You were moved by the grief of others and by the death of Your beloved friend. You experienced real emotion. You were human, and yet God. You chose this place in all of its sin; You chose earth—for me. You left heaven where there are no tears to come dwell here with us. You walked in our shoes. You hurt like we hurt. Thank You for that. Thank You for crying so I know You understand when I cry.

When Jesus saw her weeping, and the Jews who had come along with her
also weeping, he was deeply moved in spirit and troubled. "Where have
you laid him?" he asked. "Come and see, Lord," they replied. Jesus wept.

JOHN 11:33–35 NIV

Resisting Sin as a Result of Anger

I get angry, Lord. I know I can't hide it from You. You have seen it and heard it. You know all about my emotions—even the ones that aren't so sweet. The lesson You have for me in Ephesians is not that I would never get angry; it's that I wouldn't sin as a result of my anger. Tame my anger, Lord. Help me to snuff it out while it's just a spark, before it catches hold and becomes a wild and raging fire.

"In your anger do not sin": Do not let the sun go down while you are still angry, and do not give the devil a foothold.
EPHESIANS 4:26–27 NIV

The Comfort of the Holy Spirit

Lord, I am an emotional creature. I was created to experience emotions. I feel deeply. I rejoice and laugh. I also hurt and cry. It's just part of being human. It's who I am. At times, I mourn. I weep in deep grief over someone or something lost. I experience grief when I lose a loved one. I feel it when I lose a long-held dream. When something that means so much is taken from me, it is natural that I would grieve. Comfort me in such times, Lord.

"Blessed are those who mourn, for they will be comforted."
MATTHEW 5:4 NIV

_____

_____

_____

_____

_____

_____

_____

_____

_____

_____

_____

_____

_____

_____

It Is Well with My Soul

Father God, it is well with my soul. My body and mind are connected. They really can't be considered separately, because one affects the other so greatly. Thank You that I have found the secret to being at peace on the inside, regardless of my outward circumstances. The apostle Paul wrote that he had learned to be content in any circumstances, and I pray the same is true in my life.

> *Dear friend, I pray that you may enjoy good health and that all*
> *may go well with you, even as your soul is getting along well.*
> 3 JOHN 2 NIV

Self-Control

Dear God, thank You for promising me that I don't have to fear. I have been given a spirit of power, love, and self-control. I have power over my emotions in the name of Jesus. I can control how I react when I am tapped into Your power source. I find that if I'm not spending time in the Word and in prayer, I am less likely to respond calmly when I'm hit with a stressful situation. Thank You that You have put Your power in me.

God did not give us a spirit that makes us afraid
but a spirit of power and love and self-control.
2 TIMOTHY 1:7 NCV

Different Gifts

God, I love the way the Holy Spirit works. We are all gifted, yet in so many different ways. May my gifts be seen, and may they be used for the common good of Your people. Thank You for the gifts You have blessed me with, and help me to recognize the responsibility that comes with my strengths and abilities.

There are different kinds of gifts, but they are all from the same Spirit. There are different ways to serve but the same Lord to serve. And there are different ways that God works through people but the same God. God works in all of us in everything we do. Something from the Spirit can be seen in each person, for the common good.
1 CORINTHIANS 12:4–7 NCV

Bearing Fruit

Heavenly Father, I want to bear fruit for Your Kingdom. I don't want to try to do things in my own strength any longer. I have talents and abilities, but when I become proud—thinking how good I am and how much I can do for You—I am instantly taken down a notch. There is nothing in and of myself that is pleasing to You, Lord. I need You every moment of every hour in order to bear fruit. And so I must abide in You. Keep me close to Your side, Father. Never let me stray.

"I am the vine, and you are the branches. If any remain in me and I remain in them, they produce much fruit. But without me they can do nothing."
JOHN 15:5 NCV

Work vs. Rest

Sometimes, Father, I grow weary. I work and strive and try to accomplish so much. I use my gifts. I serve. I join the choir or a committee. I go on a mission trip. I hone in on my gifts, and then I use them for Your glory. But, in doing so, I often wear myself out. I know exhaustion isn't Your plan for me. Help me to strike the right balance between serving and resting, between using my gifts and simply finding solace in Your presence.

"Come to me, all of you who are tired and have heavy loads, and I will give you rest. Accept my teachings and learn from me, because I am gentle and humble in spirit, and you will find rest for your lives."
MATTHEW 11:28–29 NCV

_____

_____

_____

_____

_____

_____

_____

_____

_____

_____

_____

Resisting Pride in my Strengths

Heavenly Father, sometimes I am proud of the things I do well. It's like there's a motor inside, propelling me to do better than others. While I know it's good to be motivated and driven, please keep me from growing prideful. The gifts and abilities I have been blessed with are for Your glory, not mine. Allow me to use my gifts well and to learn and grow—not for self-glory but in honor of my King.

Don't praise yourself. Let someone else do it. Let the praise
come from a stranger and not from your own mouth.
PROVERBS 27:2 NCV

_____

_____

_____

_____

_____

_____

_____

_____

_____

_____

_____

_____

_____

Focus on the Present

Heavenly Father, I worry too much. You've told me not to worry about tomorrow but to focus on what You are doing today—in this hour, in this very moment. I could dwell on all the "what ifs" of life, or I can choose to lay them down at Your feet. There is no use in pondering all the possibilities. This kind of thinking leads to gloom and doom. Remind me to savor the serenity of walking through life with a Savior who will never leave or forsake me.

"Give your entire attention to what God is doing right now, and don't get worked up about what may or may not happen tomorrow. God will help you deal with whatever hard things come up when the time comes."
MATTHEW 6:34 MSG

God Protects Me

Lord, I am unsure about the future. There are so many question marks where there used to be periods! Everything seemed clear and so secure, but now the unknown has invaded and I am at a standstill, not knowing what to do. I need Your reassurance that You are with me. You guard me and protect me because I am Yours. Thank You for the promise that You will never let me go.

The Lord will protect you from all dangers; he will guard your life.
The Lord will guard you as you come and go, both now and forever.
PSALM 121:7–8 NCV

_____

_____

_____

_____

_____

_____

_____

_____

_____

_____

_____

_____

_____

God Has Great Plans for Me

Father God, I cannot see what lies ahead, but why do I assume so often that it's something bad? Your word refreshes me today. It promises me that no eye has seen, no ear has heard, no human mind has conceived the things You have prepared for those who love You. To think that You have such wonderful and wild plans for me! I can rest easy, remembering that the future—my future—is in Your capable hands.

However, as it is written: "What no eye has seen, what no
ear has heard, and what no human mind has conceived"—
the things God has prepared for those who love him.
1 Corinthians 2:9 niv

A Father

God, help me remember that You're my Father. A heavenly Father—One who has unlimited resources and power and One who has infinitely more love than any great earthly dad. When Satan tempts me to view You with suspicion, help me to remember that his goal is my utter destruction. Lord, fill my heart with the truth that You love me perfectly and have only the best in mind for me. In fact, You want to embrace me, bless me, and give me heaven as my inheritance. What a wonderful Father You are!

As a father has compassion on his children,
so the LORD has compassion on those who fear him.
PSALM 103:13 NIV

_____

_____

_____

_____

_____

_____

_____

_____

_____

_____

Difficult People

Dear Lord, I ask You to help me be patient and kind today. The Bible speaks about long-suffering. That's what I need as I deal with difficult people and irritating situations. Whether it's squabbling children or rude drivers or harried clerks, I know there will be those today who will irk me. In those moments when I want to scream, help me remember to forbear and forgive. It's just so easy to react, but help me instead to deliberately choose my response. I'm depending on Your power, Father.

Bear with each other and forgive one another
if any of you has a grievance against someone.
COLOSSIANS 3:13 NIV

Love

Heavenly Father, I want love to look like 1 Corinthians 13 in my household. Help me to love with patience. When my family members frustrate me, help me to hold my tongue. Help me not to be jealous. Truth be told, I sometimes think others have it easier than I do. I am juggling so many roles. . . . I feel like I have to be Super Woman, and I begin to hold grudges. Tame this emotion in me, Father.

Love is patient, love is kind. It does not envy, it does not boast,
it is not proud. It does not dishonor others, it is not self-seeking,
it is not easily angered, it keeps no record of wrongs. Love does
not delight in evil but rejoices with the truth. It always protects,
always trusts, always hopes, always perseveres. Love never fails.
1 Corinthians 13:4–8 niv

_____

_____

_____

_____

_____

_____

_____

_____

_____

_____

_____

Keep Me

Dear Father, in the scurry of life, I often forget to be thankful for important things. So many times You've shielded my family from physical harm, and I didn't know it until later. And I'm sure I don't even know about all those moments when You've guarded us from spiritual danger. Although we are the apple of Your eye, I realize we're not immune to trauma and disaster; You won't remove the effects of the curse until the right time comes. But for now, I'm grateful that You care about us and that the only way for something to touch us is after it's passed Your gentle inspection.

Keep me as the apple of the eye,
hide me under the shadow of thy wings.
PSALM 17:8 KJV

A Peaceful Home

Dear God, make my home a haven for my family and for all who come through its doors. It is so much more than just walls to us. It is where we laugh and cry. It is a shelter from the storms of life. It is where we gather to eat our meals and sleep at night. We work and play here. We want this home to honor You. Father, as we raise our family, I ask a special blessing on this home. I ask that they would know it is a safe place for them. Thank You for our home, and I pray our family feels stable and loved here always.

My people will live in peaceful places and
in safe homes and in calm places of rest.
ISAIAH 32:18 NCV

_____

_____

_____

_____

_____

_____

_____

_____

_____

_____

A Quiet Rest

Lord, we all find great blessings when in community with others, enjoying those times when we are with people. But I need Your help to embrace solitude too. Let me see the value in spending some time alone, giving my mind time to decompress, refreshing my spirit in the quiet. Not only do I need to spend quiet time with You in personal worship, but I also need to incorporate into my daily routine those pockets of time when the music is off and the computer is down. Help me make times of quiet my quest.

"In quietness and confidence shall be your strength."
ISAIAH 30:15 NKJV

The Simple Life

God, *simplicity* is a buzzword today. It seems everyone wants "simple" in some fashion. Perhaps it's because life has become too complicated for many of us; we yearn for a more laid-back lifestyle. Lord, I need to simplify my goals in my relationships and my work. Doing so will help me to have a more laser-like focus. And in my spiritual life, a little simplifying might be good too. Instead of trying to conquer large portions of scripture daily, help me to focus on a few verses, allowing me to steadily grow in understanding. Lord, help me to keep simple goals and a simple faith as I simply live for You.

> *Aspire to lead a quiet life, to mind your own*
> *business, and to work with your own hands.*
> 1 THESSALONIANS 4:11 NKJV

Legacy

God, what kind of legacy am I leaving? I want to be remembered as more than a woman who dressed nicely, had a great family, and went to church. I want to be remembered for the way I invested myself in the lives of others. After all, love is the only lasting thing on this earth, something that will remain when I am physically gone but living with You in eternity. Lord, let my legacy be wrapped up in serving others in love.

Prophecy and speaking in unknown languages and special
knowledge will become useless. But love will last forever!
1 CORINTHIANS 13:8 NLT

A God of Process

Father God, so many things are instantaneous in this world. From fast food to instant credit, we can satisfy our penchant for immediate gratification at every juncture. But I have to keep reminding myself that You often work by process. When it comes to doing the work You're doing in me, You use the steady maturing of Your Word within me to make me more like Jesus. You, the Master Gardener, water the seeds, prune the unnecessary limbs, and watch over me carefully as the fruit of my life continues to ripen. Instead of being impatient, I am to revel in Your timely and tender loving care.

But grow in grace, and in the knowledge
of our Lord and Saviour Jesus Christ.
2 PETER 3:18 KJV

Protection from Greed

Heavenly Father, thank You for blessing me financially. Thank You for my job and for the ability to pay my bills. Thank You for providing for my family. Help me to always see money as merely a resource and not a treasure to be hoarded. I want to use all of my resources, including my financial resources, for Your Kingdom.

For the love of money is a root of all kinds of evil.
Some people, eager for money, have wandered from
the faith and pierced themselves with many griefs.
1 Timothy 6:10 niv

Treasures in Heaven

Heavenly Father, I pray that You would help me keep my priorities straight when it comes to my finances. I could work my life away sticking more money in the bank. I could save it all and hoard it for a rainy day, but that rainy day may never come. I can't take the cash with me to heaven. . .so help me instead to store up treasures in heaven.

"Do not store up for yourselves treasures on earth, where moths and vermin destroy, and where thieves break in and steal. But store up for yourselves treasures in heaven, where moths and vermin do not destroy, and where thieves do not break in and steal."
MATTHEW 6:19–20 NIV

_____

_____

_____

_____

_____

_____

_____

_____

_____

_____

_____

_____

_____

Serve God, Not Money

Heavenly Father, You are my master. You are my Lord. I want to follow in Your footsteps and walk in Your ways. I see those who chase after money. They have made money their god. They worship it and seek it. They devour it when they find it. And, or them, there is never enough. Thank You for the deep peace I find in knowing that You are my God and that money is merely a tool You provide.

"No one can serve two masters. Either you will hate the one and love the other, or you will be devoted to the one and despise the other. You cannot serve both God and money."
MATTHEW 6:24 NIV

An Extravagant Gift

Heavenly Father, the disciples saw this woman's gift as a waste. She, who poured expensive perfume on Your head, was expressing her great love for You. She was anointing You with it. She had saved the best for her Lord. And yet, she was scolded for her extravagant gift. But You stopped them. You told Your followers that she had done the right thing. Show me that even though sometimes it might appear more practical to use money in a certain way, You may place a call on me that is unique.

While Jesus was in Bethany in the home of Simon the Leper,
a woman came to him with an alabaster jar of very expensive
perfume, which she poured on his head as he was reclining at the table.
MATTHEW 26:6–7 NIV

Courage to Face Change

God, change is scary. I was used to the old normal, but now there is a new normal. But it's not quite "normal" to me yet! I pray that I will find courage and strength to face the changes in my life. I need to sense Your nearness at this time. As I step out of my comfort zone, I ask that You would provide a peace that passes all understanding.

> *"Be strong and courageous. Do not be afraid or terrified because of them, for the LORD your God goes with you; he will never leave you nor forsake you."*
> DEUTERONOMY 31:6 NIV

Jesus Never Changes

Jesus, You are always the same. You have not changed. When everything around me is altered, You remain. You are steadfast. The same yesterday, today, and tomorrow. You are good. You are above all things and before all things. You hold all things together. Help me to dwell on these truths and to rest in You.

Jesus Christ is the same yesterday and today and forever.
HEBREWS 13:8 NIV

_____

_____

_____

_____

_____

_____

_____

_____

_____

_____

_____

_____

_____

_____

_____

_____

_____

Do Not Lose Heart

God, this change is tough. It feels like I might not make it through. It's overwhelming to me. I feel, at times, that You are requiring too much of me. I have faced transition before, but this time I just don't know that I can make it to the other side. Your Word tells me not to lose heart. Your Word assures me that You are there, right in the midst of this change that seems to be too much for me to handle. Renew me day by day, Lord.

Therefore, we do not lose heart. Though outwardly we are wasting away, yet inwardly we are being renewed day by day. For our light and momentary troubles are achieving for us an eternal glory that far outweighs them all.
2 CORINTHIANS 4:16–17 NIV

God Is with Me

I am up against a challenge, Father. I feel so small in its shadow. This is one of those times when I want to lean back into Your chest and listen to Your heartbeat. It beats for me, Lord, I know. Like an earthly father who wants nothing more than to protect his children from harm, You long to protect me. You are my God. You have more strength than all the earthly fathers of this world combined. With You, I have no reason to fear.

So do not fear, for I am with you; do not be dismayed,
for I am your God. I will strengthen you and help you;
I will uphold you with my righteous right hand.
ISAIAH 41:10 NIV

Peace in the Face of Struggle

Jesus, You are the Prince of Peace. And I need Your peace as I face this struggle. It is greater than me; but I know it has nothing on You! You told me that this world would have trouble. Up to this point, I have not known real trouble. But now it lies across my path like a boulder, and I have no idea how to move it. Whether You remove the trial or lead me through it, I ask for peace along the way. Thank You for always being with me.

"I have told you these things, so that in me you may have peace. In this world you will have trouble. But take heart! I have overcome the world."
JOHN 16:33 NIV

Casting My Cares on Him

Lord, I give You my cares and concerns. I offer this challenge to You as a sacrifice on the altar. I need You to sustain me. I need You to uphold me. I am weary from the struggle; I have no more strength. I am through trying to face this on my own. There are battles waging for my soul in the spiritual realms. And this is one of them. Fight for me, Jesus. I trust in You.

Cast your cares on the LORD and he will sustain you;
he will never let the righteous be shaken.
PSALM 55:22 NIV

_____

_____

_____

_____

_____

_____

_____

_____

_____

_____

_____

_____

_____

_____

Trials Are Gifts

God, this trial is stronger than I am. It is testing me in ways I have never been tested before. I am challenged at all sides, and I don't know what to do. Strengthen my faith in this time of difficulty, I pray. Walk with me. Take me *through* it, even though it would be so much easier to find a short-cut *around* it. Thank You for assuring me that You will be with me. I am ready to tackle this challenge with You—we can do it together!

Consider it a sheer gift, friends, when tests and challenges come at you
from all sides. You know that under pressure, your faith-life is forced
into the open and shows its true colors. So don't try to get out of anything
prematurely. Let it do its work so you become mature and well-developed.
JAMES 1:2–4 MSG

All Things Work Together for Good

Heavenly Father, remind me today that *all things* work together for good in the lives of those who love You. I love how this verse in scripture does not say that *some* things work together for good. It doesn't say *most* things. It says very clearly that *all things* in my life work together for good. This includes my disappointments and my failures. You are using all things together for my good. Thank You for that, Lord. It brings me peace in the midst of disappointment.

And we know that in all things God works for the good of those who love him, who have been called according to his purpose.
ROMANS 8:28 NIV

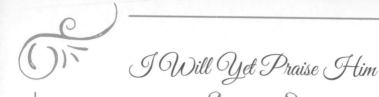

I Will Yet Praise Him

Dear Heavenly Father, I am so depressed. What I had hoped for has not come to pass. My dream is crushed. My heart is broken. My disappointment wells up inside and shows itself through tears. I am so distressed. And yet, in moments of clarity, I can see that even now You are God and You are in control. I will praise You even now. For You are my Savior.

Why, my soul, are you downcast? Why so disturbed within me?
Put your hope in God, for I will yet praise him, my Savior and my God.
PSALM 42:11 NIV

Walk by Faith

Dear Jesus, I will walk by faith through this disappointment. I will face this difficulty head-on and won't back down. I will remember all You have shown me in the light while I walk through the darkness. You have revealed to me that You are the Son of God. Give me the grace to walk in the light that I have been given for this day. Help me, Jesus, to walk by faith.

For we walk by faith, not by sight.
2 CORINTHIANS 5:7 ESV

Nothing Shall Separate Me from God

God, I am thankful for the peace I have in You. I am comforted when I read in Your Word that You will never leave me. If You are for me, it doesn't matter who else is against me. You are the God of the universe, and You are on my side. You are my Father. Distress is not my end game. I am a winner because I am on Your team.

What then shall we say to these things? If God is for us, who can be against us? . . . Who shall separate us from the love of Christ? Shall tribulation, or distress, or persecution, or famine, or nakedness, or danger, or sword?
ROMANS 8:31, 35 ESV

Everlasting God

God, You never grow weary. I am so tired of being tired. You are the Creator. I am merely the created. You never run out of power. I am spent. You are strong. I am weak. The good news for me is that I have chosen to wait upon the Lord. In this time of disappointment and heartache, I cry out to You. Help me to mount up with wings like eagles and soar.

They who wait for the LORD shall renew their strength;
they shall mount up with wings like eagles; they shall
run and not be weary; they shall walk and not faint.
ISAIAH 40:31 ESV

_____

_____

_____

_____

_____

_____

_____

_____

_____

_____

_____

_____

God's Mercies Are New Every Day

God, Your mercies are new every morning. I haven't made the best decisions in the past, and it has caused me some heartache, but today is a new day. Each day You give me a clean slate. I wake up singing of Your love. It envelops me and reminds me that I am not the sum of what I have done. I am saved by the blood of Jesus.

But I will sing of your strength, in the morning I will sing of your love; for you are my fortress, my refuge in times of trouble.
PSALM 59:16 NIV

New Life

Dear God, it's truly a miracle. I have been born again. Nicodemus didn't understand this concept. He thought Jesus meant that a man would truly be born of his mother's womb a second time. However, I understand the concept and even beyond that. I will live by faith in Christ, who made this new life possible for me. I recognize that I am not saved by works but by grace and that I cannot boast in my salvation. I owe it all to Christ.

"I have been crucified with Christ and I no longer live, but Christ lives in me. The life I now live in the body, I live by faith in the Son of God, who loved me and gave himself for me. I do not set aside the grace of God, for if righteousness could be gained through the law, Christ died for nothing!"

GALATIANS 2:20–21 NIV

He Forgets My Past Sin

Dear Heavenly Father, I know that You tell me You have forgotten my sin. So why do I keep reminding You of it? You tell me that you have cast it as far as the east is from the west. You see us as righteous once we are saved. I ask that You would remind me of Your goodness and of Your unfailing love for me.

Do not remember the sins of my youth and my rebellious ways;
according to your love remember me, for you, LORD, are good.
PSALM 25: 7 NIV

Blessings of the Present

God, I remember the words to an old song: "Count your blessings. Name them one by one. Count your blessings. See what God has done. Count your blessings. Count your blessings. Count your many blessings. See what God has done!" Sometimes I forget to do this. Please help me move forward. I don't want to dwell in the past and miss what You have for me today.

Don't ask, "Why was life better in the 'good old days'?"
It is not wise to ask such questions.
ECCLESIASTES 7:10 NCV

Maturing in Faith

Heavenly Father, You have prepared me for this time. This is my time. Each day that I live is ordained by You. You decided when I was to be born, and You led me to Jesus at just the right time. You opened my eyes spiritually. You saved me. As I live out this life, I pray that my faith will grow. I am ready to serve. Show me how You want to use me, Lord.

When I was a child, I talked like a child, I thought like a child, I reasoned like a child. When I became a man, I stopped those childish ways.
1 CORINTHIANS 13:11 NCV

_____

_____

_____

_____

_____

_____

_____

_____

_____

_____

_____

_____

_____

Comfort in the Lord

God of all comfort, I come before You grief-stricken. My heart hurts. I need You to reach down and fill me with supernatural peace. I don't understand this loss. How could it be? And yet, each day I awake to find that it was not a nightmare. This person I loved is really gone. Father, I call out to You. I ache from head to toe. I find comfort when I read in Your Word that those who mourn are blessed, for they shall be comforted. I love You, Lord. Thank You for comforting me in my time of grief.

Blessed are those who mourn, for they shall be comforted.
MATTHEW 5:4 NKJV

_____

_____

_____

_____

_____

_____

_____

_____

_____

_____

_____

Comforting Others Who Grieve

God, help me to comfort those who grieve. I have been there. I have felt the numbness and the shock of loss. I have been shaken by grief. Remind me that the greatest comfort I can offer comes not through words but through showing up and just being there. Blessed are those who mourn. They shall be comforted. Help me to be part of that comfort, Lord.

Blessed be the God and Father of our Lord Jesus Christ, the Father of mercies and God of all comfort, who comforts us in all our affliction, so that we may be able to comfort those who are in any affliction, with the comfort with which we ourselves are comforted by God. For as we share abundantly in Christ's sufferings, so through Christ we share abundantly in comfort too.
2 CORINTHIANS 1:3–6 ESV

In Christ, I Can Do All Things

I can do all things, Lord, through You. You strengthen me. You lift me up when I feel I can't go on. Where I see only one set of footprints in the sand, as the poem goes, it is then that You are carrying me. How I need You to carry me today. Grief zaps my energy. I find it hard to concentrate. I must rely on Your strength, for I truly have no resources of my own. Because Christ lives in my heart, I can press on. I will lie down and rest in peace; and when I awake, I will find enough power to face another day.

I can do all things through him who strengthens me.
PHILIPPIANS 4:13 ESV

Mustard Seed Faith

I want to please you with my faith the way the great men and women of the Bible did. But I keep coming up short. I have but a mustard seed portion of faith to bring to You. I ask You to multiply it. I ask You to grow it. You tell me in Your Word that I can do great things with even a small amount of faith. I trust this to be true, but I ask You to make me a woman of greater faith.

He said to them, "Because of your little faith. For truly,
I say to you, if you have faith like a grain of mustard seed,
you will say to this mountain, 'Move from here to there,'
and it will move, and nothing will be impossible for you."
MATTHEW 17:20 ESV

God's Word Grows My Faith

God, thank You for Your Word. All scripture is breathed by You. It teaches me. I benefit from reading it. The words jump off the pages. They correct me when I am wrong. They train me in righteousness so that I might know the right roads to take and the right decisions to make. I want to honor You in all I do. God, I am confident that as I study Your Word, my faith will grow. I will be competent to serve You, using my gifts for Your glory. Bless me, Father, as I seek to grow in my faith.

All Scripture is breathed out by God and profitable for teaching,
for reproof, for correction, and for training in righteousness,
that the man of God may be complete, equipped for every good work.
2 Timothy 3:16–17 esv

_____

_____

_____

_____

_____

_____

_____

_____

_____

_____

_____

Faith in God, Not Man

God, I am often tempted to place my faith in men instead of where it belongs—in You. I trust in those around me and almost make them my gods at times. Certainly I want to please my employer, but my boss is not my God. Certainly I hope I can trust friends and family members, but my ultimate trust must be in my Lord. Give me discernment, Father, to see when I am trusting too greatly in man and not enough in You.

That your faith might not rest in the
wisdom of men but in the power of God.
1 Corinthians 2:5 esv

Faith and Works

God, I show my faith through my works. The two go hand in hand. I cannot say I have faith and then just sit there and not do anything about it. Help me to never live in such a hypocritical manner. I find great peace when I am living out my faith. It requires something of me. It requires sacrifice. Draw me close and teach me how to have more faith each day of my life.

But someone will say, "You have faith and I have works." Show me your faith apart from your works, and I will show you my faith by my works.
JAMES 2:18 ESV

_____

_____

_____

_____

_____

_____

_____

_____

_____

_____

_____

_____

_____

God Is Faithful

Heavenly Father, I am not so unlike the disciples, am I? I know You as the One who rebuked the sea, and yet I do not trust You to calm the storms in my life. Give me greater faith, I pray. In times when I rely on my faith, I feel such peace. I am comforted to know I serve a God who always comes through. You will calm the storms in my life or You will carry me through them. Either way, You are faithful.

"Peace! Be still!" And the wind ceased, and there was a great calm.
He said to them, "Why are you so afraid? Have you still no faith?"
And they were filled with great fear and said to one another,
"Who then is this, that even the wind and the sea obey him?"
MARK 4:39–41 ESV

Remain Faithful to God Regardless of Circumstances

Father, Daniel and his friends were bold in negative circumstances. The king told them to worship a gold statue instead of You, the One true God. The king threatened to throw them into the blazing furnace. Even so, these men did not cower. They stood firm in their faith. They would have no other god before You. They would not let their circumstances dictate their faithfulness. Let it be so of me, Lord, regardless of what comes my way.

"If you throw us into the blazing furnace, the God we serve is able to save us from the furnace. He will save us from your power, O king. But even if God does not save us, we want you, O king, to know this: We will not serve your gods or worship the gold statue you have set up."
DANIEL 3:17–18 NCV

_____

_____

_____

_____

_____

_____

_____

_____

Love God

God, regardless of my circumstances, I am called to love You with all my heart, soul, strength, and mind. I am called to love my neighbor as myself. So in times of rejoicing and victory, Lord, I will love You. And in times of want, I will love You just as much. I don't want my faith to be swayed by the winds of change. No matter where I find myself, may I always be found faithful.

And he answered, "You shall love the Lord your God with all your heart and with all your soul and with all your strength and with all your mind, and your neighbor as yourself."
LUKE 10:27 ESV

Serenity in Suffering

Jesus, You suffered. You were persecuted. You were betrayed. You hung on a cross between two thieves to die a painful death. You had done nothing wrong to deserve crucifixion and yet, You hung there for me. You suffered in my place. And now I am called to suffer. There is hope beyond suffering. This is not the end but only the beginning. Allow me to suffer graciously. Allow me to rise above my circumstances.

This is what you were called to do, because Christ suffered for
you and gave you an example to follow. So you should do as he did.
1 PETER 2:21 NCV

God Will Show Up

God, You are never too early, and You are never too late. My circumstances are not great right now. I find myself in need. I have met with times that I never knew would come. I lived in plenty, but now I know what it means to live in want. I don't know where the money will come from and how the bills will be paid. God, You are greater than these circumstances. You are stronger. You are higher.

But as for me, I am poor and needy; may the Lord think of me.
You are my help and my deliverer; you are my God, do not delay.
PSALM 40:17 NIV

_____

_____

_____

_____

_____

_____

_____

_____

_____

_____

_____

Peace in Any Circumstance

Heavenly Father, I love You. I love Your Word. It is a light unto my path. It sheds light into the dark recesses of my mind. It gives instruction and correction. It comforts and guides. I love Your law. I seek to obey Your commands and walk in Your ways. I know that when I do so, my life is filled with peace, regardless of my outward circumstances. No set of circumstances has the power to steal my joy unless I allow it. I choose joy. I choose Jesus. I choose life.

Great peace have those who love your law,
and nothing can make them stumble.
PSALM 119:165 NIV

_____

_____

_____

_____

_____

_____

_____

_____

_____

_____

_____

_____

_____

_____

The Promise of Eternity

God, Job was a faithful servant. He endured many trials and tribulations, yet he remained true to his faith. I don't know how he did it, but I pray for faith like Job's. I pray that in any circumstance, I will remain true to You. Regardless of how bad it gets, I have the hope of heaven. I have the promise of eternity. So if disease should steal my health or mental well-being or strength, I will cling to my faith. I know that Jesus lives and that I will spend eternity with Him.

I know that my redeemer lives, and that in the end he will stand on the earth. And after my skin has been destroyed, yet in my flesh I will see God; I myself will see him with my own eyes— I, and not another. How my heart yearns within me!
JOB 19:25–27 NIV

Focus on Jesus

God of Peace, meet me here. I am weary from my day, and I do not see relief in sight. This situation has exhausted me. I am tired, but I am not defeated. I find rest in You. I find comfort in knowing that You are God. I will focus on Your ways. I know that there is great peace to be found for those whose hearts are steadfast. I desire such peace.

You will keep in perfect peace those whose
minds are steadfast, because they trust in you.
ISAIAH 26:3 NIV

Like a River

God, I really have no idea where I am going. The future is very unclear to me. I take solace in the fact that You are in control. I want to be a channel of water controlled by You. Direct the flow. Lead me where You want me to go. Use me as You use a river, Lord. Use me to nourish and to strengthen others. Use me to help them move from one place to another. Use me to provide refreshment to their souls.

Good leadership is a channel of water controlled by GOD;
he directs it to whatever ends he chooses.
PROVERBS 21:1 MSG

Blessed, and a Blessing

God of Abraham, Isaac, and Jacob. . .God of my forefathers. . . God who is with me, who made me, who sees me, who longs to bless me. I come before You. I ask You to bless me and to help me be a blessing to others. May my superiors see Jesus in me. May I look like Jesus in my workplace. I pray that if You raise me up, I will always remember the One who took me there. You alone deserve all honor and glory and praise.

Now the LORD said to Abram. . . "I will make of you a great nation, and I will bless you and make your name great, so that you will be a blessing. I will bless those who bless you. . .and in you all the families of the earth shall be blessed."
GENESIS 12:1–3 ESV

God Can Do Anything

God, You have great plans for me. They are greater than my wildest dreams or my highest aspirations. Please help me to continue to work hard and set goals. Give me motivation to succeed and to grow. I have so many dreams for my life that I hope to see come true. But remind me that it is not "me, myself, and I" who make my dreams come true. It is all because of You.

Now to him who is able to do far more abundantly than all that we ask or think, according to the power at work within us.
EPHESIANS 3:20 ESV

_____

_____

_____

_____

_____

_____

_____

_____

_____

_____

_____

_____

God Establishes My Steps

You are the Master Planner. You are the One who establishes my steps regardless of the dreams I may have. Thank You, God, that I can trust You. You will never take me down a road that is not best for me. You know the plans You have for me, and they are for my good. I find great serenity in the knowledge that You, my God, are in control.

In their hearts humans plan their course,
but the Lord establishes their steps.
PROVERBS 16:9 NIV

Family and Friends

God, sometimes I feel lonely. Thank You for my family members who always have a way of lifting my spirits. Thank You also for friends who have become like family over the years. This world can be a cruel place. Help me to be aware of those in my circles who may not have friends and family. Especially at the holidays, Lord, help me to be mindful of those who may experience loneliness. May there always be room in my home for one more to join us!

God sets the lonely in families, he leads out the prisoners
with singing; but the rebellious live in a sun-scorched land.
Psalm 68:6 niv

Serenity in Solitude

When I am lonely, Lord, I look to You. I find moments of solitude to worship and to pray. Jesus withdrew from the crowds that followed Him. He found "lonely" places. He sought them out. Teach me to do the same. Show me that it is important for me to sometimes be alone and read Your Word. There is serenity to be found in solitude.

But Jesus often withdrew to lonely places and prayed.
LUKE 5:16 NIV

The Christian Is Never Alone

Father God, I feel lonely. I need Your comfort and Your companionship. I love that because I am Your child, I never have to truly be alone. It would be frightening to do this life all alone. Instead, I have You near—always. You are at my side. You are the One true God, and I am so thankful that I never have to be alone.

Turn to me and be gracious to me, for I am lonely and afflicted.
PSALM 25:16 NIV

The Lord Keeps Me Safe

You alone, Lord, are my safety. You are my portion. You are my God. I can find peace even if I am all alone because You are always with me. There is serenity to be found in being a believer in Christ. All the days of my life I will walk with goodness and mercy following me, because I belong to the Good Shepherd, the Great I Am, the Sovereign God of the universe. I am never truly alone because You are with me. I find great peace in this.

In peace I will lie down and sleep, for you alone,
LORD, make me dwell in safety.
PSALM 4:8 NIV

Peace in Wisdom

God, I long for wisdom. I seek it and find it when I ask You to bless me with it. I know that it is better to find wisdom than to possess great riches. It is more precious than the finest of jewels. Nothing I desire compares with my desire for wisdom. Thank You for the peace that I find in wisdom. Thank You for blessing me with wisdom when I ask You for it with my whole heart.

Blessed is the one who finds wisdom, and the one who gets understanding, for the gain from her is better than gain from silver and her profit better than gold. She is more precious than jewels. . . . Long life is in her right hand; in her left hand are riches and honor. Her ways are ways of pleasantness, and all her paths are peace.
PROVERBS 3:13–17 ESV

Wisdom from Above

Your wisdom is true wisdom, God. So many people scurry around here on earth. They think they have found the keys to success. They promise the same success to others. If you just buy this product. . . If you just take this class. . . If you just become part of this program. . . But these are empty pursuits. They lead to nowhere fast. There is nothing false or misleading in true wisdom. Give me discernment, Father, as I seek wisdom. Help me to find the peace that comes with wisdom from above.

But the wisdom from above is first pure, then peaceable, gentle,
open to reason, full of mercy and good fruits, impartial and sincere.
JAMES 3:17 ESV

Avoiding Foolishness

Heavenly Father, make me wise. Give me a cautious spirit that recognizes the evil one. Help me to avoid the pitfalls Satan would love for me to fall into. Help me to be careful and to have wise judgment. May my conversations be honorable and my word choice pure. Father, always set before me a glimpse into the future. Please bless me with the serenity found in wise choices.

One who is wise is cautious and turns away
from evil, but a fool is reckless and careless.
PROVERBS 14:16 ESV

Christ Alone

God, please help me to be strong. There are so many voices calling out to me, offering their own brands of wisdom. Father, may I always follow Christ and Christ alone. Let no one take me captive by philosophy or empty deceit. I will seek You and You alone. Please bless my life with wisdom and a calm assurance that is found only in following hard after Christ.

See to it that no one takes you captive by philosophy and
empty deceit, according to human tradition, according to the
elemental spirits of the world, and not according to Christ.
COLOSSIANS 2:8 ESV

Walking with the Wise

God, thank You for wise friends. Thank You for the relatives I have in my life who pursue wisdom and walk closely with You. Thank You for the Christian leaders in my circle. They lead me well in the way of wisdom. Provide godly counsel at times when it is needed in my life. Thank You for the peace that comes through walking with those who walk with You.

Walk with the wise and become wise, for a companion of fools suffers harm. Trouble pursues the sinner, but the righteous are rewarded with good things. A good person leaves an inheritance for their children's children, but a sinner's wealth is stored up for the righteous.
PROVERBS 13:20–22 NIV

Fear of the Lord Is the Beginning of Wisdom

Lord, I have a healthy fear of You. It is not a fear that shudders in Your presence or cowers when You draw near. You are a God of love, and I am Your beloved child. But I have a fear of You, just the same. It is a respect. It is a reverence. You are my heavenly Father. I come before You with respect. The beginning of wisdom is the fear of the Lord. Please bless me with wisdom, God. I long to know You better.

Give instruction to a wise man, and he will be still wiser; teach a righteous man, and he will increase in learning. The fear of the Lord is the beginning of wisdom. . . . For by me. . .years will be added to your life.
PROVERBS 9:9–11 ESV

Do Not Brag in Wisdom

Lord, thank You that I can know You. While I don't know You fully, I am seeking to know You more each day. I study Your scriptures. I fellowship with Your people. May I boast only in You. You are good. You are loyal, and You act in love. You do what is right. You set things straight. One day every knee shall bow and every tongue confess that You are Lord. Until then, may I delight in the bits of wisdom You graciously bestow upon me.

> *"If you brag, brag of this and this only: That you understand and know me. I'm GOD, and I act in loyal love. I do what's right and set things right and fair, and delight in those who do the same things. These are my trademarks."*
> JEREMIAH 9:23–24 MSG

_____

_____

_____

_____

_____

_____

_____

_____

_____

_____

A Daughter of the King

Heavenly Father, thank You for adopting me into Your family. Thank You that I am truly a daughter of the King of kings. You call me Your heir, Your child, Your beloved daughter. I will walk with You all the days of my life. As Your child, help me to walk in peaceful ways. Make me one who is patient and kind. Give me the ability, I pray, to identify others who need to know You. I want everyone I come in contact with to know what it means to be a child of God.

Yet to all who did receive him, to those who believed in his name, he gave the right to become children of God.

JOHN 1:12 NIV

My Motives

God, You see my heart. You see more than appearances; You see motives. You are sovereign. . . . You see all and know all. There is no hiding my motives from You. Help me to be true to who I say I am in Christ. May my motives and desires reflect who You are. Just as a child resembles a biological parent, I want to look like You. When others look at me, I want them to see a heart that passionately pursues Christ.

You may believe you are doing right,
but the LORD judges your reasons.
PROVERBS 21:2 NCV

_____

_____

_____

_____

_____

_____

_____

_____

_____

_____

_____

A New Creation

Heavenly Father, I thank You for the peace I find in knowing that I am a new creation in Jesus Christ! His death on the cross and my faith in Him have made me a brand-new person with a heart that has been cleansed from all unrighteousness. Though I continue to sin and mess up royally at times, You always stand ready to forgive. Help me to please and honor You in all I do and say. Remind me that when I feel defeated, I am more than enough in Your eyes because of the One who gave His all that I might be found sinless and blameless before You.

Therefore, if anyone is in Christ, the new creation has come: The old has gone, the new is here!
2 CORINTHIANS 5:17 NIV

From Death to Life

God, I stand amazed that You would choose me as Your own. I have been buried with Christ in baptism and raised to walk in newness of life. I am a new creation in Jesus, and I can walk and talk with Him as my Savior and friend! Just as Jesus died, my old life has passed away. Just as He rose after three days, I have been raised as His disciple. Thank You for new life. Thank You for saving me!

We were therefore buried with him through baptism into death in order that, just as Christ was raised from the dead through the glory of the Father, we too may live a new life.
ROMANS 6:4 NIV

From Darkness to Light

God, the story of Saul's conversion always inspires me. Saul was a persecutor of Christians. He was as far from You as anyone could imagine. And yet, You chose him. Saul became Paul, the great apostle of the Lord Jesus Christ. He went from murderer to messenger in a flash. He laid down his weapons for the Word of God; he stopped killing and started evangelizing. I want to be identified as one who walks closely with You, Lord. I want to be known as a bold disciple of Christ. Give me strength all the days of my life to live for You.

As he neared Damascus on his journey,
suddenly a light from heaven flashed around him.
ACTS 9:3 NIV

Be of One Mind

Father, I long for serenity in my relationships. I want to be like-minded with those in my closest circles. Even among my Christian brothers and sisters, there is much disunity. Help me to be a peacemaker not a wave maker. Give me opportunities to shine for You, and help me to be seen as one who lives at peace with others. Replace my critical eyes and tongue with vision and words straight from Your holy heart.

Finally, brothers and sisters, rejoice! Strive for full restoration,
encourage one another, be of one mind, live in peace.
And the God of love and peace will be with you.
2 Corinthians 13:11 niv

Love One Another

Holy God, no one has ever seen You. You are too holy for us to look upon. And yet, I have seen You in others. I have seen You in teachers in my church who give of themselves tirelessly, serving and spreading Your Word to all who will listen. I pray my words and actions would show that Jesus Christ has taken up residence in my heart and that I truly live for Him. I want to point others to You all of my days, Father. Teach me to love as You love.

No one has ever seen God; but if we love one another,
God lives in us and his love is made complete in us.
1 JOHN 4:12 NIV

Generosity in Relationships

Heavenly Father, show me ways I can be more generous in my relationships. I want to be a safe person for those who are closest in my life. I want to provide a listening ear and a shoulder to cry on when needed. Give me that type of generous and loving spirit so that I might be at peace in all of my relationships. Even more, I pray that I am a blessing to all those with whom I come in contact.

A generous person will prosper; whoever
refreshes others will be refreshed.
PROVERBS 11:25 NIV

_____

_____

_____

_____

_____

_____

_____

_____

_____

_____

_____

_____

_____

A Kind Woman

Kind God, give me a kind heart. Help me to commit random acts of kindness today that will bless my family and friends. When I am busy at work, help me to keep my cool and respond with grace and patience to others' demands. At the end of a long day, give me a gentle spirit as I deal with my family. Help me to listen and to nurture each member of my family with kindness, for I know this pleases You.

A kindhearted woman gains honor,
but ruthless men gain only wealth.
PROVERBS 11:16 NIV

Moment by Moment

Father in heaven, I have a tendency to try to live a week or month at a time. It's difficult for me to limit myself to one day, one hour, one minute. But that's how You want me to live. You know that projecting into the future causes me to wonder and worry about things that haven't happened yet. You also know that I can't be any good to anyone if my head is in the clouds, thinking about the future. So help me live in today—that's all I have at the moment.

"Does He not see my ways, and count all my steps?"
Job 31:4 NKJV

Near to God

God, draw near to me, I pray. Just as I long for human touch and connection, I long (even more so) for a connection with You. You are my Creator, my Savior, my very best friend. Your Word tells me that when I draw near to You, You are there. In times that I begin to stray, reach out to me, Father. Never let me go. Draw me close to You as a mother holds her young. I want to be in the safest place of all—in Your arms.

Come near to God and he will come near to you. Wash your hands, you sinners, and purify your hearts, you double-minded.
JAMES 4:8 NIV

_____

_____

_____

_____

_____

_____

_____

_____

_____

_____

Faithful Worker

God, I admit sometimes I don't give it my all at work. Most of the time I do. Sometimes I even go overboard, working too many hours and neglecting other areas of my life. I am not all that I should be in my workplace. I know that when I do my very best, others around me take notice. Help me, Father, to be faithful to You even in my work. Grant me the ability and desire to work as if I am working for You every single day.

Servants, do what you're told by your earthly masters. And don't just do the minimum that will get you by. Do your best. Work from the heart for your real Master, for God, confident that you'll get paid in full when you come into your inheritance. Keep in mind always that the ultimate Master you're serving is Christ.
COLOSSIANS 3:23–25 MSG

Work and Rest

Heavenly Father, I read in Ecclesiastes that there is a time for everything. A time to work and a time to rest. When You created the earth, You set a model for us to follow. You worked and then You rested. Grant me wisdom in this, Lord. Help me to work hard and to please You in all that I do in the workplace. Help me also to know when it is time to rest.

By the seventh day God had finished his work. On the seventh day he rested from all his work. God blessed the seventh day. He made it a Holy Day because on that day he rested from his work, all the creating God had done. This is the story of how it all started, of Heaven and Earth when they were created.
GENESIS 2:2–4 MSG

_____

_____

_____

_____

_____

_____

_____

_____

_____

_____

Provision

Heavenly Father, You have always provided for me. You meet my needs so wonderfully. The Bible says that You even care for the birds of the air, providing the food they need. . .and so how much more will you provide for us—Your children! I thank You for my job that helps to provide money for my family. I ask You to keep me grounded and focused on the work at hand. Please bless me in my work each day, and help me to honor You with not only my work but my attitude about it as well.

A hard worker has plenty of food, but a person
who chases fantasies has no sense.
PROVERBS 12:11 NLT

Peace in My Work

Thank You, heavenly Father, that I can lay my head on my pillow at night and rest. There is great peace to be found in knowing that I am working hard to help provide for my family. I am not interested in being rich. I know that my job is a gift from You, and I pray I will always remember to treat it as such. I ask that You would help me to rest easy in the knowledge that I am working hard and honoring my God.

People who work hard sleep well, whether they eat
little or much. But the rich seldom get a good night's sleep.
ECCLESIASTES 5:12 NLT

Praying Protection over My Church

Heavenly Father, I ask for Your protection over Your Church. Just as Saul, before his conversion, was seeking to destroy the church, so many outside forces seek to harm Christians today. Guide us to see that we must bond together and not be torn apart. Nothing will destroy Your Church. You declare that there will always be a remnant of Your people. Let my church be one that pleases You in all we do, and help us to live and worship and serve in harmony with one another.

But Saul was going everywhere to destroy the church. He went from house to house, dragging out both men and women to throw them into prison.
ACTS 8:3 NLT

_____

_____

_____

_____

_____

_____

_____

_____

_____

_____

_____

A Praying Church

Help us, God, to be a praying church. It is easy in this day and age to think we can do things by our own strength. We have so much technology at our fingertips to make lights and music glorious. We have resources and money to do things within the walls of our church. You are all that matters. If we do not emphasize prayer in our church, we are missing the mark entirely. Help us to stop working long enough to pray. Remind us to pray earnestly for the body of Christ.

But while Peter was in prison,
the church prayed very earnestly for him.
ACTS 12:5 NLT

_____

_____

_____

_____

_____

_____

_____

_____

_____

_____

Church Growth

God, thank You for my church. I love the people who gather there together in Your name. We have become a family—the body of Christ in this community. There are people whom I can count on and people who can count on me. It feels good to belong, to be a part of something bigger than myself. Help us, Father, to grow—both in our faith and in numbers.

So the churches were strengthened in
their faith and grew larger every day.
ACTS 16:5 NLT

Truth, Like Treasure

God, like precious jewels stored in a treasure chest, I will store Your teachings in my heart of hearts. May I always have Your commands in my thoughts, and may I honor You in all that I do as a result. May loyalty and kindness be like a bull's-eye target that I wake up each day aiming to hit. Hold me close, Father, and whisper Your truth and Your love over me.

My child, never forget the things I have taught you. Store my commands in your heart. If you do this, you will live many years, and your life will be satisfying. Never let loyalty and kindness leave you! Tie them around your neck as a reminder. Write them deep within your heart.

PROVERBS 3:1–3 NLT

_____

_____

_____

_____

_____

_____

_____

_____

_____

_____

_____

Direct My Paths

Heavenly Father, I trust You. Help me to trust You even more. I want to trust in You so fully that when I come to a fork in the road and have a decision to make, I instantly—on impulse—look to You. I am just a mere human, a woman. I don't have the wisdom to know even a fraction of what You know. I want to walk on paths of righteousness. I want to honor You, my God. I ask for wisdom.

Trust in the LORD with all your heart; do not depend on your own understanding. Seek his will in all you do, and he will show you which path to take.
PROVERBS 3:5–6 NLT

Think on Heavenly Things

Heavenly Father, I know that this earth is not my home. I am but a visitor here, an alien, one who is passing through but who does not truly belong. My identity is in You. My old life has gone, and my new life is hidden with my Jesus in You. Help me, I pray, to put any sinful ways to rest. I want my life to be a vessel of worship for You, my King.

Think about the things of heaven, not the things of earth. For you died to this life, and your real life is hidden with Christ in God. . . . So put to death the sinful, earthly things lurking within you. Have nothing to do with sexual immorality, impurity, lust, and evil desires. Don't be greedy, for a greedy person is an idolater, worshiping the things of this world.
COLOSSIANS 3:2–5 NLT

Focus on God

Heavenly Father, please help me fix my gaze on You. I know that whatever I am focused on is where I will end up. If I focus on the world, the world will consume me. If I set You before me as my target, my goal, and my destination, You will be where I end up! I want to honor You and live for You. I find the greatest peace in times when I know I am right in the midst of Your will, Father. Keep me always focused on You.

Let your eyes look straight ahead; fix your gaze directly before you.
PROVERBS 4:25 NIV

Thinking of Others

God, please keep me from selfish thinking. Help me to think of others before myself, never as less than or not as important. In my humanity, I look out for number one. But I am not a slave to my humanity any longer. I have Christ in my heart. I am a new creation. I can, in His power, look beyond myself and my desires and even my needs. I can think of those around me. I can see their struggles. I can feel their pain. May I follow in His footsteps. May I think of others first.

Don't be selfish; don't try to impress others. Be humble, thinking of others as better than yourselves. Don't look out only for your own interests, but take an interest in others, too.
Philippians 2:3–4 NLT

Take Every Thought Captive

God, I will choose today to take every thought captive to my Jesus. I know that as my thought life goes, so goes my spiritual life. Please don't let my thoughts lead me to unholy places. Keep me from conflict and arguments. Keep me from sin, I pray. As soon as a thought begins to creep into my mind that may not be a righteous thought, may I recognize it and take it captive to Christ. May Christ be the center of my existence. Help me to truly surrender my thoughts to You.

We demolish arguments and every pretension that sets itself up against the knowledge of God, and we take captive every thought to make it obedient to Christ.
2 CORINTHIANS 10:5 NIV

_____

_____

_____

_____

_____

_____

_____

_____

_____

_____

Anxious for Nothing

God, my emotions get the best of me sometimes. I let worry creep in and take over when I shouldn't. Remind me that You are always there, and You hear my prayers. Please help me not to let my emotions take control, but give me the presence of mind to take every thought captive to Christ. When I am under stress, I will take in a deep breath and let it out slowly. I will exhale, knowing that You have me in the palm of Your hand.

Do not be anxious about anything, but in every situation,
by prayer and petition, with thanksgiving, present your requests
to God. And the peace of God, which transcends all understanding,
will guard your hearts and your minds in Christ Jesus.
PHILIPPIANS 4:6–7 NIV

It Is Well with My Soul

Father God, it is well with my soul. My body and mind are connected. They really can't be considered separately, because one affects the other so greatly. Thank You that I have found the secret to being at peace on the inside, regardless of my outward circumstances. The apostle Paul wrote that he had learned to be content in any circumstance, and I pray the same is true in my life. Thank You, Lord, that with Jesus in my heart I can truly say it is well with my soul.

Dear friend, I pray that you may enjoy good health and that
all may go well with you, even as your soul is getting along well.
3 John 2 niv

In Christ's Strength

God, I may be better at some things than others. We all are. I have my strengths and weaknesses just like the next woman. But the Bible tells me that I can do all things through Christ, who strengthens me. *All things.* I think this means that anything I am called to do, I will have the strength to accomplish. On my own, I can do nothing. With Jesus, it is quite the opposite. He is a game changer. He makes the ending of my story so much more magnificent than the beginning. I can do *all things* through my Jesus.

I can do all things through him who strengthens me.
PHILIPPIANS 4:13 ESV

In His Image

Father God, I am created in Your image. You made everything in the world, but Your final masterpiece was mankind. Thank You, Father, for making me in Your image and saving me through Your Son. I am humbly aware that I have many weaknesses, but I thank You that I am seen as enough by my Father. You see me through a Jesus lens, and I am Your precious daughter. What a blessing, God.

So God created man in his own image, in the image of God he created him; male and female he created them.
GENESIS 1:27 ESV

_____

_____

_____

_____

_____

_____

_____

_____

_____

_____

_____

_____

_____

Power in Weakness

God of all power, thank You for being my power source. When I am weak, You are strong. Just as the children's song says: "Jesus loves me. This I know—for the Bible tells me so. Little ones to Him belong. They are weak, but He is strong. Yes, Jesus loves me!" What a blessing to know that I am not expected to or required to be the best at everything. I can tap into the power available to me through Christ anytime and in any place. I surrender my weaknesses to You, Lord, for in You I am strong.

He gives strength to those who are tired and
more power to those who are weak.
ISAIAH 40:29 NCV

One Body, Many Parts

God, help me to remember that while I am not good at everything, I have been given gifts. And I am to use them for Your glory. The body of Christ is an amazing thing. I look around and see those who are so very different from me. It's difficult not to be envious of others' talents and abilities. Many have been gifted with a beautiful singing voice or the gift of mercy, while those are not my specialities! But I need to remember that You are the One who chose how I should be gifted. I will focus today on my strengths, not my weaknesses.

Together you are the body of Christ,
and each one of you is a part of that body.
1 Corinthians 12:27 ncv

Come to Jesus

I come to You, Lord Jesus. That is the first step. I come before You now in this quiet moment. As I begin this day, calm my spirit. There is work that must be done today. But even as I work, I can find rest in You. Ease the tension and stress in me, Lord, as only You can do. Thank You for a sense of peace. Amen.

Come unto me, all ye that labour and are
heavy laden, and I will give you rest.
MATTHEW 11:28 KJV

Don't Worry

God, I have been told that tomorrow has enough trouble of its own. I shouldn't borrow trouble. Remind me again of this truth. You tell me not to worry; worrying does no good. Instead, I should lay down my cares at Your feet and trust in You that everything will be okay. You are so strong. You are so good. You are with me and for me, and You never leave. Stay with me now, Lord. Comfort me. I need to sense Your presence.

"Don't worry and say, 'What will we eat?' or 'What will we drink?' or 'What will we wear?' The people who don't know God keep trying to get these things, and your Father in heaven knows you need them. Seek first God's kingdom and what God wants. Then all your other needs will be met as well."
MATTHEW 6:31–34 NCV

The Plans God Has for Me

Lord, You know the plans You have for me. You see the future even though it is so unclear to me. I stand here very uncertain of what tomorrow holds, but You are never uncertain. You know the number of hairs on my head. I find great serenity in knowing You go before me—that You know the plans—because You are the One who made them. I love You, Lord.

"For I know the plans I have for you," declares the LORD, "plans to prosper you and not to harm you, plans to give you hope and a future."
JEREMIAH 29:11 NIV

_____

_____

_____

_____

_____

_____

_____

_____

_____

_____

_____

_____

Love Deeply

God, I read in Your Word that You are Love. I personally have experienced Your eternal love, Your amazing grace. And yet I struggle, at times, to love my husband. It was all so easy in the beginning. Help me to love my husband deeply, for love covers a multitude of sins. He is not perfect; nor am I! But I will love him well. And in doing so, I will love You, Lord.

Above all, love each other deeply,
because love covers over a multitude of sins.
1 PETER 4:8 NIV

_____

_____

_____

_____

_____

_____

_____

_____

_____

_____

_____

_____

_____

Becoming One

Marriage is a mystery, God—a mystery of two becoming one. I sometimes feel the strongest bond with my husband. I understand that we are one now. However, I often feel very, very separate from him. I must seek to love him even as I love myself—for he is the other part of my heart. Thank You for my husband, Father, and for the unity we share. May our bond always be one that honors You.

And the two will become one flesh.
So they are no longer two, but one flesh.
MARK 10:8 NIV

_____

_____

_____

_____

_____

_____

_____

_____

_____

_____

_____

_____

_____

_____

Filled with Praise

Father, complaining is on Your list of dislikes. Because the ancient Israelites griped in the desert, they had to endure forty years of wandering. I don't want to be like them. When I'm tempted to complain, remind me of their story. It would be easy to moan and groan today, but You don't ask us to do what is easy. You ask us to do only what is right. So help me to focus on praise right now. Thank You.

Let my mouth be filled with Your
praise and with Your glory all the day.
PSALM 71:8 NKJV

Rest for a While

God, there's nothing like a few days of relaxation! I'm glad You built the structure of our world. On the seventh day of creation, You rested. And You even designed laws for the Old Testament Hebrews so they would have to rest. (You knew those workaholics would ignore the Sabbath if the consequences weren't serious!) And now, I have the chance to take some time off for rest. Because of You, I am going to enjoy it to the fullest!

Then Jesus said, "Let's go off by ourselves
to a quiet place and rest awhile."
MARK 6:31 NLT

Why?

Heavenly Father, I'm sometimes like a child. I want to know *why*. But, like a wise father, You don't always give an answer. You know that, with my human understanding, I can't comprehend Your sovereign ways or grasp the purpose of Your decisions. So You withhold some information from me because it's not good for me to know. Help me be content to let You run the universe. I'll probably always ask questions, but I trust You. So, even amid the mysteries of life, I rest assured, secured, and adored, knowing You mean the best for me.

> *"The secret things belong to the LORD our God, but those things which are revealed belong to us and to our children forever."*
> DEUTERONOMY 29:29 NKJV

Guidance in Financial Decisions

God, I know many people who are after the get-rich-quick schemes. They scramble to try to make a fast buck; but in the end, I know it will only lead to destruction and debt. Help me to always be wise in how I make, save, and spend money. Everything that I have comes from You. Remind me of this and allow me to never hold too tightly to any earthly thing—including money.

Dishonest money dwindles away, but whoever
gathers money little by little makes it grow.
PROVERBS 13:11 NIV

The Love of Money

God, I love You. I love Your world and Your people. I love sunsets and sunrises painted by Your hands—masterpieces for Your children to enjoy. I love Your Word, full of wisdom and truth, which teaches and corrects me every day of my life. I love Jesus, who died upon the cross for my sins. I love my family and my friends, people hand-chosen by You to enrich my life. But I do not love money. If a person loves money, he or she always wants more of it. Help me to always to be content and thankful for whatever money You bestow upon me. And help me to use it wisely.

Whoever loves money never has enough; whoever loves wealth is never satisfied with their income. This too is meaningless.
ECCLESIASTES 5:10 NIV

Financial Peace

Heavenly Father, I pray for guidance in my financial decisions. Give me wisdom, I pray, to know whether to take out a loan, how to pay off a debt quickly, and other matters of money I face daily. God, I know that it is best to keep short tabs. I know that it is best to pay cash. Show me how to operate according to these principles. A debt-free life offers great peace and serenity.

Do not be one who shakes hands in pledge or puts up security for debts; if you lack the means to pay, your very bed will be snatched from under you.
PROVERBS 22:26–27 NIV

_____

_____

_____

_____

_____

_____

_____

_____

_____

_____

_____

_____

_____

Debt-Free Living

Heavenly Father, I haven't always been wise with money. I pray that You will guide me and show me ways to allocate my money so that I can pay off debt. I truly want to be debt free so that I may honor You in this area of my life. It seems so hard to live within my means, but I know it can be done if I put my mind to it. I pray for guidance that I might get out of debt quickly. Thank You, Father, for hearing my prayer. I know You will help me.

Let no debt remain outstanding, except the continuing debt to love one another, for whoever loves others has fulfilled the law.
ROMANS 13:8 NIV

A Time for Change

There is a time for everything, God. You make this so clear in Your Word. This change in my life was not unexpected to You. You had it in Your plans. You knew I would struggle with it, but You also know the outcome. You see a year. . .five years. . . ten years into my future. Help me to realize I serve a sovereign God who has not made a mistake nor taken His hand off my life, even for a brief second. You are in this change, Lord. Help me to embrace it.

There is a time for everything, and a season
for every activity under the heavens.
ECCLESIASTES 3:1 NIV

_____
_____
_____
_____
_____
_____
_____
_____
_____
_____
_____
_____
_____

Hope in the Lord

Father God, You are faithful. Through all the changes I must endure, You are true. You do not change like shifting shadows. You remain. You hold on to me. You sing over me as I lay my head on my pillow and trust in You to see me through the night. This time is not easy. I am in new and unfamiliar territory. Be gracious, Lord. See me through this change as only You can.

Yet this I call to mind and therefore I have hope: Because of the Lord's great love we are not consumed, for his compassions never fail. They are new every morning; great is your faithfulness.
LAMENTATIONS 3:21–23 NIV

Focused on the Lord

God, I remember the story of Your disciple who set out to walk upon the water. As long as he kept his eyes on You, he walked across the surface of the sea. But when he lost his focus, he began to sink. He had to keep his eyes on You in order to be successful. I will keep my eyes on You. I refuse to let Satan win. I will not be shaken. I will rely on You, my God, and in Your strength, I will prevail.

I keep my eyes always on the LORD. With him
at my right hand, I will not be shaken.
PSALM 16:8 NIV

Help from the Lord

I don't know what I'm doing, Lord. I'm up against a trial that has me stumped. I have tried every angle and keep coming up empty. So I come to You. I lay my burden at Your feet because You care for me. You know the way out of this mess I have gotten myself entangled in, and I need You to work. Boldly, I pray for Your assistance. I thank You in advance, because I know that help is on the way.

If you don't know what you're doing, pray to the Father. He loves to help. You'll get his help, and won't be condescended to when you ask for it. Ask boldly, believingly, without a second thought. People who "worry their prayers" are like wind-whipped waves.
JAMES 1:5–8 MSG

_____

_____

_____

_____

_____

_____

_____

_____

_____

Resist the Devil

Heavenly Father, I pray that I would not let the devil have a foothold in this situation. I am struggling, but I am not destroyed. I will not fall prey to the evil one, who would love to see me give up on You. I find my hope in the living God. Make me aware of his sneaky schemes. When I hear a message in my mind that tells me I am not strong enough, help me to stop right then and take that thought captive to Jesus. I am strong enough—not in and of myself—but through Christ, who gives me strength.

*Be sober-minded; be watchful. Your adversary the devil
prowls around like a roaring lion, seeking someone to devour.*
1 Peter 5:8 esv

God Restores the Years Eaten by Locusts

God, I've wasted a lot of years. I wish I could get them back. I was not who I should've been. I wasn't walking with You. It pains me to think of all that wasted time. Time I could have spent in Your Word. Time I could have spent serving You. I feel behind in my study of the Bible when I compare myself to others my age. God, You are the restorer of wasted things. You bring beauty from ashes. In Jesus' name, I commit my past to You, asking You to redeem it.

I will restore to you the years that the swarming locust
has eaten, the hopper, the destroyer, and the cutter,
my great army, which I sent among you.
Joel 2:25 esv

Forgetting the Past

Heavenly Father, I can relate to the apostle Paul. I started out on a really bad track but have seen the light. I am walking with Jesus; and while my past really stinks, I still have a bright future ahead of me. Help me, God, to truly forget what is behind and strain toward what is ahead. I am so blessed in my new life to be walking with Jesus. Please help me to never return to my old sin nature.

Brothers and sisters, I do not consider myself yet to have taken hold of it. But one thing I do: Forgetting what is behind and straining toward what is ahead, I press on toward the goal to win the prize for which God has called me heavenward in Christ Jesus.
PHILIPPIANS 3:13–14 NIV

_____

_____

_____

_____

_____

_____

_____

_____

_____

_____

Live in the Present

Lord, I can't stop living in the past. I dig up old memories, and they drag me down. I heard once that if you live in the past, you will miss the present; and therefore, you will have no future. I think this is true. I am seeing it played out in my life. I am afraid to take risks, Lord. Take me to the place of healing, whether it is through counseling or writing a letter to someone from my past. . .or whatever path You see fit. I love You, Father, and I thank You for helping me to find peace with my past.

The LORD says, "Forget what happened before,
and do not think about the past."
ISAIAH 43:18 NCV

No More Tears

Heavenly Father, I have experienced a deep loss. The grief overwhelms me. And yet it comes in waves. On my darkest days when grief will not let up, I rest in the knowledge that one day everything will be made right. I look forward to that, God. I find peace in knowing this life is not all there is for me. One day there will truly be no more tears.

"He will wipe away every tear from their eyes, and there will be no more death, sadness, crying, or pain, because all the old ways are gone."
REVELATION 21:4 NCV

The Dead in Christ Shall Rise

Heavenly Father, the promises in Your Word are clear. Heaven is real, and believers in Christ will spend eternity there. It sounds like a scene from a movie, Father, with awesome special effects. And yet, it is in Your Word. And it is true! I cannot imagine how it will feel when that trumpet sounds. To see the dead in Christ alive again and meeting Jesus in the sky! And it will last for all eternity! In Jesus' name, I pray.

For the Lord himself will descend from heaven with a cry of command. . . . And the dead in Christ will rise first. Then we who are alive, who are left, will be caught up together with them in the clouds to meet the Lord in the air, and so we will always be with the Lord.
1 Thessalonians 4:16–17 esv

Jesus Destroyed Death

Heavenly Father, I am so thankful that Jesus defeated death. The sting of death has no more power in the life of a Christian. When death comes, we simply pass over into eternity with You in heaven. The hope of heaven eases the pain of grief. Find me here in my grief, Father. For even though I know the promises, I am hurting. Sing over me. Comfort me. Help me, Lord, as I walk through sorrow.

But it is now shown to us by the coming of our Savior Christ Jesus. He destroyed death, and through the Good News he showed us the way to have life that cannot be destroyed.
2 TIMOTHY 1:10 NCV

Standing Out as One Who Is Wise

God, I want to stand out as a woman full of Your wisdom. There are people who have walked with You for a long time. I see them in my church and in my community, and I recognize them as Your saints. God, I want to grow in wisdom. Please give me wisdom from above. Give me insight. Show me Your perspective. Let me see people and events around me through Your lens rather than my own, which is so limited.

Who is like the wise? And who knows the interpretation of a thing? A man's wisdom makes his face shine, and the hardness of his face is changed.
ECCLESIASTES 8:1 ESV

_____

_____

_____

_____

_____

_____

_____

_____

_____

_____

_____

_____

God Sees the Lonely

Heavenly Father, You are so aware of our needs. You do not sit on your throne in heaven and forget about Your children. Your eyes wander to and fro across the land. You see us in our loneliness. Be with me now, I pray. Comfort me. Provide relationships for me that will fill up my lonely heart. I am often lonely, sometimes even in a crowd. Please bring serenity to my solitude, I pray.

A father to the fatherless, a defender of widows, is God in his holy dwelling. God sets the lonely in families, he leads out the prisoners with singing; but the rebellious live in a sun-scorched land.
PSALM 68:5–6 NIV

_____

_____

_____

_____

_____

_____

_____

_____

_____

_____

_____

Choose Friends Wisely

Lord, I don't need a lot of friends. I need a few who stick close and love me well. I look to Your example in this. When You were on earth, You walked closely with the Twelve. They were Your disciples. They followed You. Thank You for blessing me with a few just as You had a few. I can love the world and be in it, but not of it. My security is not found in numbers. My security can only be found in You. Thank You for a close friend who loves me well. Help me to always have such a friend.

One who has unreliable friends soon comes to ruin,
but there is a friend who sticks closer than a brother.
PROVERBS 18:24 NIV

Praying for God's Will

Lord, Your name is holy, and Your ways are great. I come before You and pray as Jesus taught. I ask that You come quickly. This earth is not my home. Reveal to me the needs in the world. Show me how my life can make a difference here. I love You, Father, and I am so thankful that I get to be a small part of what You want to do in this world. In Jesus' name, I pray for Your will to be done in my life.

Your kingdom come, your will be done, on earth as it is in heaven.
MATTHEW 6:10 NIV

_____

_____

_____

_____

_____

_____

_____

_____

_____

_____

_____

_____

If the Lord Wills

Heavenly Father, I do not know what tomorrow will bring. This doesn't frighten me, though, because I know the One who holds tomorrow in His hands. Who am I to make plans? You are God. You never change. I ask You to remind me that all my plans should be filtered through Your loving fingers. I only desire Your will, Father. If my dreams are outside of that, please reveal that to me.

Come now, you who say, "Today or tomorrow we will go into such and such a town and spend a year there and trade and make a profit"— yet you do not know what tomorrow will bring. What is your life? For you are a mist that appears for a little time and then vanishes. Instead you ought to say, "If the Lord wills, we will live and do this or that."
JAMES 4:13–16 ESV

Committing My Work to God

God, I commit my work to You. I have so many goals, but I know that none of them can be reached in my own strength. If You are not in my plans, my plans have no point. I ask You to take the goals that I have designed and the dreams in my mind and alter them to conform to Your will. Establish my plans, Father. Bless my hard work.

Commit your work to the LORD,
and your plans will be established.
PROVERBS 16:3 ESV

Faith in Jesus

Heavenly Father, so many people say they "believe," but they don't believe in You. Some have faith in themselves. They believe that they are strong. They don't see that they are weak and that only through You are they able to be strengthened. No one comes to the Father but through Jesus. Thank You for my faith that promises me eternal life.

Truly, truly, I say to you, whoever believes has eternal life.
JOHN 6:47 ESV

Faith in God, Not Man

God, I am often tempted to place my faith in men instead of where it belongs—in You. I trust in those around me and almost make them my gods at times. I am saved by grace through faith in Jesus, and I want to have a greater, stronger faith. You have come through for me again and again. Teach me to build altars at these places where You have blessed me. I want to live by faith, knowing that You will always come through for me.

That your faith might not rest in the
wisdom of men but in the power of God.
1 Corinthians 2:5 esv

Faith. . .the Unseen

God, this world focuses on things that can be seen. Money, fashion, entertainment. The spiritual realm is much the opposite. I must learn to focus on what is unseen—this is faith. Faith is the assurance of things hoped for. Strengthen my faith, I pray.

Now faith is the assurance of things hoped for,
the conviction of things not seen.
HEBREWS 11:1 ESV

Jesus Heals

My heart is broken, Lord. I have lost someone so dear to me. My heart wells up with grief, and I can think of nothing else. Nothing seems right in the world now. Father, I need You in these days. I need You every hour. Be merciful with me, I pray. Thank You for the comfort of knowing You care and that You promise to take care of me.

He heals the brokenhearted and binds up their wounds.
PSALM 147:3 ESV

_____

_____

_____

_____

_____

_____

_____

_____

_____

_____

_____

_____

_____

_____

God Cares When I Grieve

Abba Father, Daddy, You catch my tears. You save them in a bottle. You care. Each tear I cry hurts You. Your heart is a Father's heart, tender toward Your child. Keeping our feelings inside is never good. God, I love You, and I thank You for caring for me. Help me to cast this grief at the foot of Your throne. Help me to trade my burden for Yours, which is lighter. I surrender my grief to You.

You have kept count of my tossings; put my
tears in your bottle. Are they not in your book?
PSALM 56:8 ESV

_____

_____

_____

_____

_____

_____

_____

_____

_____

_____

_____

_____

Discouraged, but Not in Despair

Heavenly Father, thank You for being my Rock. You are there, and I instantly turn to You when I am in distress. I may face persecution, but I will never be abandoned. I may fall down, but I will get up again in Your strength. I am not destroyed. I may have some battle scars, but I will be victorious. I have Christ in my heart, and I can do all things through Him who strengthens me.

We are hard pressed on every side, but not crushed; perplexed, but not in despair; persecuted, but not abandoned; struck down, but not destroyed.
2 Corinthians 4:8–9 niv

God Hears My Cry for Help

Thank You, heavenly Father, for hearing me when I cry. Please see my hurt and heal my brokenness. Put me back together so that once again I can feel whole. I will serve You all of my days. Some days are just harder than others; I struggle to get out of bed and face the world. Help me today, Lord. Give me strength. Remind me that even in my distress, You have not forgotten me. You will see me through, and even this shall pass.

When the righteous cry for help, the LORD hears. . . . The LORD is near to the brokenhearted and saves the crushed in spirit. Many are the afflictions of the righteous, but the LORD delivers him out of them all.
PSALM 34:17–19 ESV

_____

_____

_____

_____

_____

_____

_____

_____

_____

_____

_____

The Lord Answers Me

Lord, I need You. Just as a little child calls out in the night when she is frightened, I call out to You now. There is so much peace and comfort for me in the knowledge that You are there. You are right by my side the instant that I call to You. I am facing yet another battle now. Help me in this trial. Thank You for the peace I feel just knowing we are in this together. I know I never fight alone.

When I was in trouble, I called to the LORD, and he answered me.
PSALM 120:1 NCV

The Lord Fights for Me

Heavenly Father, I think of all the trials I have faced. You have walked through them with me—day by day. You save me again and again, Father. Often, You are called upon to save me even from myself. And You always show up. You never lose a fight. You are victorious, Lord. I praise You now in advance for the victory I know You will provide in the face of yet another enemy. I am ready to go into battle with You, Father.

The LORD gives me strength and a song. He has saved me. Shouts of joy and victory come from the tents of those who do right: "The LORD has done powerful things." The power of the LORD has won the victory; with his power the LORD has done mighty things.
PSALM 118:14–16 NCV

Blessings in Change

God, I wasn't expecting to have to face a change like this right now in my life. It's certainly not what I wanted. This change may not be comfortable or easy or even welcomed, but it is going to be okay. Because You are my God, and I trust in Your ways. Your understanding is far greater than mine. In Jesus' name, I commit this change to You.

For my thoughts are not your thoughts, neither are your ways my ways, declares the Lord. For as the heavens are higher than the earth, so are my ways higher than your ways and my thoughts than your thoughts.
Isaiah 55:8–9 ESV

God Makes a Way

Lord, You are a God of the unexpected. You bring about changes we don't count on, but that are just right for us. I believe with all my heart that even if the change feels like a dead end or a wrong turn to me, there is good in it. You know the plans You have for me, and they are always in my best interest (Jeremiah 29:11). Thank You, God, for always looking out for me.

See, I am doing a new thing! Now it springs up; do you not perceive it?
I am making a way in the wilderness and streams in the wasteland.
ISAIAH 43:19 NIV

An Excellent Wife

Heavenly Father, help me to be a wife like the one described in Proverbs 31. I know my home will be a more peaceful place when it's filled with love between my husband and me. We set the tone for our family—our children look to us for an example. Sometimes I am tempted to be selfish. I look to my own needs before I notice his. I must learn to put off self and take on selflessness in order to have a strong marriage. Help me, Lord.

An excellent wife who can find? She is far more precious than jewels.
The heart of her husband trusts in her, and he will have no lack of gain.
She does him good, and not harm, all the days of her life.
PROVERBS 31:10–12 ESV

God Is with Me

Heavenly Father, I find peace when I read in Zephaniah that You will rejoice over me with singing. The Lord, my God, is with me. That is such a wonderful promise! Believers in Christ have nothing to fear because You are always fighting for us. There are battles I cannot see in the spiritual realms. You defend Your own against the evil one. As I feel myself beginning to fear the future and all of life's uncertainty, I fix my eyes again on Jesus. I see Him there on the cross, dying for my sin. That kind of love is beautifully unfathomable.

"The Lord your God is with you, the Mighty Warrior who saves.
He will take great delight in you; in his love he will no longer
rebuke you, but will rejoice over you with singing."
ZEPHANIAH 3:17 NIV

Living Free

God, the old has gone; the new has come. I am no longer a slave to sin, but I have been set free. Help me to live as one who is free. Remind me, every moment of every day, of the new identity You have blessed me with, Father. Help me to focus on Christ and never look back. There is no need to act as a slave when one has been set free!

For we know that our old self was crucified with him
so that the body ruled by sin might be done away with,
that we should no longer be slaves to sin.
ROMANS 6:6 NIV

_____

_____

_____

_____

_____

_____

_____

_____

_____

_____

_____

_____

_____

Making a Difference in my Work

Father, from the very beginning there has been work. Though my work sometimes feels mundane, help me to discover the meaning in it. Guide me to a greater understanding of all the ways I am making a difference in the world. Give me opportunities to make a Kingdom difference in my work, Lord. If there are those with whom You want me to share Christ, make it evident to me.

GOD took the Man and set him down in the Garden
of Eden to work the ground and keep it in order.
GENESIS 2:15 MSG

_____

_____

_____

_____

_____

_____

_____

_____

_____

_____

_____

_____

_____

Wisdom in My Work

Heavenly Father, I am called on to make a lot of decisions in my work. Every day there are choices to be made, and I am not always sure what's best. Give me wisdom, I pray, to make the best decisions. Help me to always consider any ethical and moral implications. Guide me to think about others and to think beyond today and into the future.

She considers a field and buys it;
out of her earnings she plants a vineyard.
PROVERBS 31:16 NIV

When Work Feels Useless

Father God, I am spent. My work wears me out, and it seems—at least some days—to serve no purpose. I don't always understand why You have kept me here in this job for so long. It feels like a dead end. Show me if and when it is time for a change. I pray that You will bring just the right people and job opportunities across my path when it's time for a change.

> *I replied, "But my work seems so useless! I have spent*
> *my strength for nothing and to no purpose. Yet I leave it*
> *all in the Lord's hand; I will trust God for my reward."*
> ISAIAH 49:4 NLT

_____

_____

_____

_____

_____

_____

_____

_____

_____

_____

_____

_____

One Spirit

Heavenly Father, I love the word *harmony*. Please bless my church always with peace and tranquility. The world seeks to tear us down, but Your Church is a place where we can build one another up instead. Give us Your eyes to see one another as precious and cherished. May we always be a Church that is known for our love, Lord. Bless us with a deep, abiding love for You as our sovereign Lord and for one another in the body of Christ.

So then, let us aim for harmony in the church and try to build each other up.
ROMANS 14:19 NLT

Unity in God's Church

Heavenly Father, may there be no divisions within my church. It isn't my church, after all. It isn't the pastor's church. It doesn't belong to us. It belongs to you. It is your church. Your Church should not look like the world with all of its strife and conflict. It should stand out as different. It should be a haven for people, not a place of hostility. May we come together as one body with one spirit. May we seek unity in the Lord Jesus above all else.

First, I hear that there are divisions among you when
you meet as a church, and to some extent I believe it.
1 CORINTHIANS 11:18 NLT

Truth in Love

Heavenly Father, to speak the truth in love is not always easy. Sometimes there are disagreements within my church. Other times, there are believers who stray and need correction. Help my church and its leaders know how to speak the truth in love. We are all sinners and lose sight of the right ways at times. I ask that we will be led always to speak the truth in love within my church. In this way we will grow more and more like Jesus, which is always our goal.

Instead, we will speak the truth in love, growing in every way more and more like Christ, who is the head of his body, the church.
Ephesians 4:15 nlt

Direct My Paths

Heavenly Father, I trust You. Help me to trust You even more. I want to trust in You so fully that when I come to a fork in the road and have a decision to make, I instantly—on impulse—look to You. This world calls out to me with many voices. It seems that everywhere I turn, I have to fight temptations to walk on paths I know lead nowhere. I want to walk on paths of righteousness. I want to honor You, my God.

Trust in the L{ord} with all your heart; do not depend
on your own understanding. Seek his will in all you do,
and he will show you which path to take.
P{ROVERBS} 3:5–6 {NLT}

Not Letting Emotions Rule over Me

God, please replace any negativity in me with a smile. I have heard it said that attitude is a little thing that makes a big difference, and I believe that to be true. When I allow circumstances to dictate my emotions, I quickly go down a road that leads to depression and sadness. But when I, instead, choose to look on the bright side, my heart is lifted and my whole self follows. Bring a peace that passes all understanding to my heart, I pray.

A happy heart makes the face cheerful, but heartache crushes the spirit.
PROVERBS 15:13 NIV

_____

_____

_____

_____

_____

_____

_____

_____

_____

_____

_____

Seek Peace and Pursue It

Heavenly Father, my emotions can lead me astray—and quickly! When I am sad or angry, I can easily go down the wrong road. I start condemning myself or others, creating burdens that we are not meant to bear. I say things I don't mean. I act in a manner that does not reflect the Gospel of Christ. Help me in these moments to stop and simply turn to You. Help me turn from evil and instead, choose what is good and right.

Turn from evil and do good; seek peace and pursue it.
PSALM 34:14 NIV

God Is Still There

God, I know You haven't left me or even looked away for one moment. I know You are still here. You are the same yesterday, today, and forever. That brings me great comfort, because right now I feel like my world has been turned upside down. I am so disappointed. I am struggling, God. I refuse to crumble at this trial. I will instead call out to You, my God. I reside in the shelter of Your presence. I rest now in Your shadow. Take from me my past with its disappointment and provide a new dream for me to hold on to, I pray.

"He is my refuge and my fortress, my God, in whom I trust." Surely he will save you from the fowler's snare and from the deadly pestilence.

PSALM 91:2–3 NIV

_____

_____

_____

_____

_____

_____

_____

_____

This Sort of Obedience

Master of sea and sky, the storm is raging fiercely around me and within. I am swamped by the waves. Where are You, Lord? I feel as though You are asleep. Forgive me for forgetting that You who created me have also redeemed me. As You call me by name and claim me as Yours, so You also call out and rebuke the wind and the sea. Open my eyes to see and to feel You at the helm, to be liberated by Your peace-producing love. Let Your great calm settle over me. Remind me what sort of God You are and how even the winds and sea obey You.

Then he rose and rebuked the winds and the sea, and
there was a great calm. And the men marveled, saying,
"What sort of man is this, that even winds and sea obey him?"
MATTHEW 8:26–27 ESV

_____

_____

_____

_____

_____

_____

_____

_____

_____

Coming as the Rain

Lord, draw near to me. May Your Word refresh my soul. I thirst for Your presence like a cooling hand on a fevered brow. I hope in Your coming; I trust that You hear my cries and know my sorrow. Many times I feel as though I can only confess these struggles internally to You. There seems to be no other brother or sister in Christ in whom I can confide. Lord, if it is Your will, raise up a body of believers who can walk beside me in this struggle, who will pray and fight with me. May I patiently wait for Your call and hope in the showers of promise.

"Let us know; let us press on to know the LORD;
how going out is sure as the dawn; he will come to us
as the showers, as the spring rains that water the earth."
HOSEA 6:3 ESV

A Bedtime Prayer

In my heart, Father God, I know You will fight for me. You are the One in control. You know where I have been, where I am right now, and where I am going. You have it all planned out. So I need to be still. I need to remember that You are God Almighty. You love me. You will not let me fall. When I close my eyes to sleep, fill my thoughts with Your Word. Set my mind on Jesus, Your Son. Reveal His presence all around me. Remind me that He protects me all through the night and never leaves my bedside. Help me rest in Christ's love and be still. Give me sweet peace, dear Lord.

"The Lord will fight for you; you need only to be still."
Exodus 14:14 niv

Jesus' Hands

I can do nothing but bow before You in awe and worship when I think about how amazing it is, Lord. You've engraved my name in the palm of Your hands. Lord Jesus, when You were crucified, with nails driven into Your palms, You remembered everyone who would ever turn to You. The scars on Your hands are a continual reminder of how much You care. Each time I think of what You endured, I remember Your indescribable love for me and that You will never forget me. It's more than my mind can comprehend, but my heart swells in adoration. I don't know the words to thank You for such amazing love, but I open myself up to You, trusting that Your name will be eternally inscribed on my life.

"See, I have engraved you on the palms of my hands; your walls are ever before me."
ISAIAH 49:16 NIV

Winning the Mind Games

Father God, I choose today to relax and settle my heart and mind. I focus my thoughts on You—on Your goodness, Your mercy, and Your love. You love me so much. You've promised to work all things together for my good because I love You. I push the negative thoughts out of my mind. I choose to fill my thoughts with Your Word and what it says about my life. I am a child of the Most High, bought with a price, and I belong to You. I am free from condemnation. Nothing can separate me from Your love. You have not given me a spirit of fear, but of power, love, and a sound mind. You have promised me peace, sweet peace. Thank You for that peace now.

Worry weighs a person down;
an encouraging word cheers a person up.
PROVERBS 12:25 NLT

Rejoice and Be Glad

Lord, You open my senses to the beauty around me: the rhythm of the steady rain, the wind's song, the majestic sight of ragged clouds racing across a stormy sky. The lightning and thunder embody Your greatness. They reflect Your authority over heaven and earth. Rejoice and be glad! Rejoice! God is good! Yes, Lord, You made this day, and just like every day, it is filled with the wonder of You. So I will not let a veil shroud my heart. I will not let gray skies bring me down. Instead, I will reflect on the goodness of You. I will reflect and be grateful and glad. Amen.

This is the day which the LORD hath made;
we will rejoice and be glad in it.
PSALM 118:24 KJV

_____

_____

_____

_____

_____

_____

_____

_____

_____

_____

Peace from God

To have real peace, I need to think on those things that please You, Father. Instead of filling my mind with images and information the world around me supplies, I need to dwell on Your goodness and the wisdom and knowledge that comes from the Holy Spirit. Increase my hunger for Your Word. Whatever I see, read, hear, or speak, let it bring You glory. For when it brings You glory, it will bring me peace. Lord, I want to be kept in perfect peace. I ask You to transform my thinking and desires. Help me trust You completely and keep my mind on You and Your Word.

Trust ye in the LORD for ever: for in the
LORD JEHOVAH is everlasting strength.
ISAIAH 26:4 KJV

Great and Mighty God

Father, give me peace in this valley while I wait. Ease my mind. Increase my faith, and enlighten me with hopeful scriptures. Make me intensely aware of Your presence. Encourage me to listen for Your voice and to recognize when You urge me to act. I know, Father, that this valley is temporary. I believe with all my heart that You have something wonderful waiting for me on the other side of the mountains. So come, great and mighty God. Come and lift me up.

The mountains melt like wax before the Lord,
before the Lord of all the earth.
Psalm 97:5 niv

Beauty for Ashes

Father, my hope is in You. I know that, despite my current state, You're taking me to a place of joy and beauty and happiness. Help me clear my tears enough to notice the sweet blessings You lay in my path. Each time I feel anxious, remind me to focus on the promises of this verse. Gladness, praise, and beauty are in store for me, along with Your never-ending love and faithfulness. Thank You for the good things You have for me. I love You, and I trust You.

He has sent me. . .to bestow on them a crown of beauty
instead of ashes, the oil of joy instead of mourning,
and a garment of praise instead of a spirit of despair.
ISAIAH 61:1, 3 NIV

Master Builder

Father, You are the Master Architect of my life. You built it, but sin and others' actions and my own choices have caused a lot of damage. But since You're the One who created me in the first place, I know You have the power to re-create and rebuild and restore what's been lost. Instead of focusing my thoughts on the destruction, help me set my mind on the current construction that's taking place. I know You're working behind the scenes to fashion something beautiful and wholesome, something even better than I can imagine. Thank You for Your divine design in my life, Father.

They will rebuild the ancient ruins and restore the places long devastated; they will renew the ruined cities that have been devastated for generations.
ISAIAH 61:4 NIV

Inexhaustible Strength

When the enemy reminds me that I can't erase my past, I will remember that You, Father, have erased my sin. You don't speak to me from the point of my past mistakes but from a place of freedom. Help me learn from my past and move forward. I am forgiven and free from condemnation. My future—today and for all eternity—is not based on how many times I failed or succeeded. It is, instead, based on my relationship with You. Thank You for forgiving me and for filling me with Your inexhaustible strength.

"The thief comes only to steal and kill and destroy.
I came that they may have life and have it abundantly."
JOHN 10:10 ESV

Come to the Waters

Help me relax in You today, Lord. When my spirit tightens in worry and stress, remind me of the abundant buffet of Your love, ready and waiting for me to partake. When I'm hungry, fill me. When I'm anxious, give me peace. And when I feel lonely and frightened, comfort me with Your presence. Thank You for loving me, Father.

"Come, all you who are thirsty, come to the waters;
and you who have no money, come, buy and eat!
Come, buy wine and milk without money and without cost."
ISAIAH 55:1 NIV

Grow My Faith

Heavenly Father, You have brought me so far. You have saved me from my sins. You have written my name in the Lamb's book of life. You have grown me in my faith. You have provided so many wonderful opportunities for me. Make me open to whatever You have planned for me. I know that, far more important than exactly what career path I take, is the way you desire to mature me in my faith. Use me, God. Alter my dreams as You see fit.

And I am sure of this, that he who began a good work in you will bring it to completion at the day of Jesus Christ.
PHILIPPIANS 1:6 ESV